Homework

Other Classmates:

2nd Series

Successful Subject Co-ordination – Christine Farmery
Parent Partnership in the Early Years –
Damien Fitzgerald
Playing Outdoors in the Early Years – Ros Garrick
Assemblies Made Easy – Victoria Kidwell
Getting Promoted – Tom Miller
ICT in the Early Years – Mark O'Hara
Creating Positive Classrooms – Mike Ollerton
Getting Organized – Angela Thody and
Derek Bowden
Physical Development in the Early Years –
Lynda Woodfield

1st Series

Lesson Planning – Graham Butt
Managing Your Classroom – Gererd Dixie
Teacher's Guide to Protecting Children – Janet Kay
Tips for Trips – Andy Leeder
Stress Busting – Michael Papworth
Every Minute Counts – Michael Papworth
Teaching Poetry – Fred Sedgwick
Running Your Tutor Group – Ian Startup
Involving Parents – Julian Stern
Marking and Assessment – Howard Tanner

Homework

Victoria Kidwell

continuum
LONDON • NEW YORK

Continuum

The Tower Building
11 York Road
London SE1 7NX

15 East 26th Street
New York
NY 10010

British Library Cataloguing-in-Publication Data
A catalogue record for this book is available from the British Library.

ISBN 0–8264–7309–1 (paperback)

Typeset by BookEns Ltd, Royston, Herts.
Printed and bound in Great Britain by
Antony Rowe Ltd, Chippenham, Wiltshire

Homework

Homework! Oh, homework!
I hate you, you stink!
I wish I could wash you
away in the sink,
if only a bomb
would explode you to bits.
Homework! Oh, homework!
You're giving me fits.

I'd rather take baths
With a maneating shark,
Or wrestle a lion
Alone in the dark,
Eat spinach and liver,
Pet ten porcupines,
Than tackle the homework
My teacher assigns.

Homework! Oh, homework!
You're last on my list,
I simply can't see, why you even exist,
If you disappeared
It would tickle me pink,
Homework! Oh, homework!
I hate you, you stink!

Jack Prelutsky

Contents

Contents

Part One

Everything You Need to Know About Homework

Introduction (and a bit of a rant!)

Children spend a minimum of six hours a day working at school. How can we justify making them spend more time doing schoolwork at home?

What's wrong with learning from real experiences in the real world? Why can't they go out with their family or friends? What's wrong with pursuing their own choice of hobby or sport in the evenings? Even talking to other family members can be highly stimulating and educational. The child would probably learn far more from a vigorous discussion than a page of trigonometry.

Mention the dreaded 'H-word' and a variety of reactions and emotions arise: fear, rage, despair and resignation, to name but a few. All too rarely is homework met with rapturous joy and exhilaration. In this age of 'edutainment' and far lower boredom thresholds, it is getting increasingly hard to deliver homework tasks that are welcomed. This is despite the incredible wealth of resources available to all concerned. The Internet has revolutionized access to information for all parties involved.

I have had the dubious privilege of approaching the subject from almost every perspective: as a former pupil (albeit last century), as an overworked teacher, as a stressed-out parent and, now, from a more comfortable distance. Phew! Before the Alzheimer's completely sets in, I'll just say that, way back in the

Homework

twentieth century, as a bone-idle, easily distracted member of the school community, I had to be cajoled every step of the way by my long-suffering parents and teachers. Modesty aside, when it came to homework avoidance, I was a professional. Later, as a teacher, I was also sometimes more than reluctant to give homework, especially when even *I* couldn't see the point of it. Often, I felt obliged to dole out tasks, purely because a badly thought-out policy was telling me I had to do so. The fire alarm may have gone off during the lesson or, perhaps, I had gone off on a particularly interesting red herring, thus rendering the homework I had planned completely meaningless or inappropriate. Now, as a parent, I often *deeply* resent the fact that my two little cherubs have to spend their evenings completing homework tasks rather than being able to go out and frolic in the pastoral idyll outside. Pages of sentences using adverbs! Ugh! *Why*? A couple of sentences would probably have done the trick!

Why this apparently irrational aversion towards homework? The answer is simple: homework for homework's sake. Grrrr! Poorly planned and badly administered homework is indeed 'a waste of paper' and 'cruelty to children', to quote my daughter.

Whatever your remit in the homework jungle, pupil, parent or teacher, there is nothing more irritating than receiving, giving or supervising (in my son's case, almost at gunpoint!) meaningless, boring and utterly unmotivating tasks. In recent years, the situation has greatly improved, largely because schools and teachers are far more accountable to the tax-paying public than we used to be. Parents seem more willing to get involved as well.

Introduction

As we all know, policies on virtually every aspect of school life (sometimes to a farcical level!) are formulated by schools' management teams. This has to be a good thing! Policies are all very well: but unless these well-meaning documents are implemented *effectively* by their authors, the unsuspecting teacher at the chalk face can find himself up the proverbial creek without a boat, let alone a paddle!

Moreover, as far as I am concerned, the most enjoyable aspect of teaching is finding creative ways to teach and reinforce one's subject. Homework plays an incredibly important role here. Teachers must be allowed to be creative and not turned into policy-regurgitating, mindless automatons. Flexibility must be incorporated into the policy itself.

Rant over! Personally, I am not *completely* convinced about the benefits of homework. However, by the look of recent government initiatives, it's here to stay.

I started researching this book with reservations and finished it feeling amazed at the resources available to teachers, pupils and parents – but still with reservations. There is definitely the potential for some cracking homework tasks out there. But, does homework demotivate purely because it's homework?

Whether you're a school manager, who is attempting to improve your school's homework strategies in a way that will benefit *everyone* (not just Ofsted), or a teacher, who is the victim of inept, pen-pushing imbeciles, I hope the following pages will help.

1

Definition of Homework

In the tradition of Miss Donald, my A-level English teacher, I am now going to 'define' my 'terms'. This may seem rather ridiculous but schools define homework in a variety of ways. I discovered this whilst 'bobbing around on' the Internet (I haven't quite reached surfing standard yet). As a reverent, tax-paying citizen, I'd better go with the government's interpretation of the term 'homework': 'any work or activities which pupils are asked to do outside school time, either on their own or with parents or carers.'

2

Research on Homework

The government's national guidelines on homework are based on research (both in the United Kingdom and abroad) into the potential benefits of homework. I was quite surprised to learn how little coordinated research there is on this much-debated issue.

Like SATs tests, a lot of this research tells us what we know already. Nevertheless, it is useful to put the government's guidelines into context.

The findings of different studies can be contradictory – it's not me – honestly!

After-school study support initiatives

These are new phenomena on the educational bandwagon. Little research has been done on their effectiveness. In general, however, they seem to be getting a good press. Only time will tell.

The 'quick fix'

There have been many recent initiatives by the government as well as by independent organizations to facilitate the completion of homework. Homework websites, telephone helplines and virtual teaching on the Internet have burgeoned.

Homework

As they are relatively new developments, it is impossible to accurately gauge their success. Children undoubtedly find them helpful. Preliminary findings, however, suggest that these 'quick fix' approaches are of limited benefit when it comes to improved academic achievement: a study in America offered 46 children from Year 6 telephone homework assistance over a period of 16 weeks. A mere 12 availed themselves of this service. There was no positive relationship between participation in the homework assistance programme and academic achievement. My own experience would also substantiate this: pupils just tend to look for an isolated piece of information, which can only be of limited benefit.

Time spent on homework

This aspect of homework has been under quite a lot of scrutiny, both nationally and abroad. It is one of the few areas in which international comparative studies have been carried out. Here are the findings:

- At secondary school level, particularly from the age of 14, there is a positive relationship between time spent on homework and achievement. However, the variance is *very small*!

- At primary school level there is *no* conclusive evidence that more time on homework leads to higher achievement.

- At primary school, *lower* achievers spend longer on their homework.

8

- At secondary school, *higher* achievers spend longer on their homework.

- Girls spend longer on their homework than boys.

- Asian students spend longer on their homework than other ethnic groups.

- Pupils doing very little or a great deal of homework are outperformed by those doing a moderate amount.

- More time on homework does *not* necessarily lead to better achievement.

Homework and pupil attitudes

I'd approach research findings on this topic rather like adult sex surveys: I would tend to question the honesty of pupils' responses, especially with regard to frequency and enjoyment! On top of this, there has been very little research done. But here goes anyway:

- Overall, pupils have positive attitudes to homework.

- Pupils feel that homework is important in helping them to do well at school.

- Pupils dislike being set 'routine' homework tasks such as finishing off class work.

- Pupils dislike activities they feel do not contribute to their learning.

- Pupils like interesting, challenging and varied tasks.

9

Homework

- Pupils like work that is clearly defined.

- Pupils greatly appreciate adequate deadlines.

- Girls are willing to spend more time on homework than boys.

- There is no discernible relationship between the amount of homework given and pupil attitudes.

- There has been negligible research into whether setting homework for primary school children has any effect on their attitudes towards studying later on.

Homework for lower-achieving pupils

- Assignments must be appropriate.

- Lower achievers need more encouragement.

- Parental involvement and communication are vital.

- Tasks should be short.

- Tasks should be relevant.

- Homework planners and diaries are of benefit.

- Self-monitoring techniques are effective.

- Teachers need to handle the issue of differentiation with sensitivity because lower achievers feel stigmatized by being given different homework from their peers.

Parental involvement in homework

- Most parents want schools to set homework.

- Homework can be a cause of conflict between parents and children.

- The younger the child, the more involved the parent.

- Cultural and socio-economic factors *do* have a bearing on parental involvement.

- There is *not* a clear relationship between the degree of parental involvement and pupils' achievement at school.

- It is possible for parents to intervene in either appropriate or inappropriate ways.

- Parental involvement in reading is not sufficient for success.

The homework environment

- Pupils who spend time on a range of after-school activities perform better at school.

- Appropriate conditions *are* essential.

- Parental encouragement *is* important.

- More time spent watching television *does* tend to mean less time on homework.

- Pupils' homework preferences relate to their home environment.

11

Homework

- Pupils' home environment relates to their pre-ferred learning style (visual, text, aural, etc).

- There are cultural and gender differences with regard to pupil preferences and their homework environment.

- Pupils learn better when given advice tailored to their individual learning style.

- There is no conclusive research on homework clubs. However, as they offer access to learning resources and an appropriate learning environ-ment, they are conducive to study.

- Individualized homework tasks do not appear to raise pupil achievement sufficiently to justify the additional time required.

Homework and parental attitudes

Research has been done on parents' thinking about homework. A study in 1995 reported five major themes:

- Concern about their child's unique characteristics as balanced with school demands.

- Questions about the appropriate level of indepen-dent work assigned to their child.

- Concerns about how they can best structure homework activities.

- Concerns about how involved they should be in helping their child with homework.

◆ Reflections about what it means to them whether they are or aren't successful at being able to help their children complete assignments.

Research carried out in 1994 noted that homework could lead to greater parental involvement in school. However, in doing this, it also accentuated the difference between higher and lower achievers. Higher achievers' parents tended to become more involved.

Research into misconceptions about homework

A report in 1996 found five widespread myths about homework:

1. The best teachers give homework regularly.

The best teachers vary assignments according to the task in hand; many teachers think that homework policies stating that homework should be given on a regular basis undermine their curricular goals and personal teaching style.

2. More homework is better than less.

The amount of homework assigned has not been proven to be a reliable indicator of increased academic performance.

3. Parents want their children to have homework.

Parents do want their children to succeed at school, but this desire cannot be interpreted to mean that they want their children to have homework if it's not going to improve their academic performance.

4. **Homework supports what children learn in school.**

Teachers give *many* reasons for setting homework; many homework assignments do *not* serve to help students reorganize and extend their learning.

5. **Homework fosters discipline and personal responsibility.**

There is little evidence to support this widely held idea; parents foster these characteristics in larger, broader ways than through doing homework.

Research into the positive and negative effects of homework

Positive effects:

- Immediate effects on achievement and understanding: better retention of factual knowledge; increased understanding; better critical thinking and concept formation; better information processing; curriculum enrichment.

- Long-term academic effects: learning encouraged during leisure time; improved attitude towards school; better study habits and skills.

- Non-academic long-term effects: greater self-direction; greater self-discipline; better time organization; more inquisitiveness; more independent problem solving.

Negative effects:

- Satiation: loss of interest in academic material; physical and emotional fatigue.

- Denial of access to leisure time: parental interference; pressure to compete and perform well.

- Cheating: copying from other students; having a tutor provide help beyond tutoring.

Homework and standardized test results

Research carried out in America indicates that the effects of homework varies according to the age of the pupil. The grades of those who received homework were compared to those who did not.

High school pupils:

- Students who received homework outperformed the others by 69 per cent.

- Time spent on homework *outside* school had greater effects than time spent *in* school.

- Achievement effects *increased* according to the *amount of time* spent on homework.

Junior high school pupils:

- Those who received homework outperformed the others by 35 per cent.

- Homework was more effective than supervized in-school study.

15

Homework

- Academic effects increased as time spent on homework increased to two hours.

- More than two hours did not increase achievement.

Elementary school pupils:

- There was no difference in performance between those given homework and those who were not.

- In-school supervized study had a greater impact on achievement than homework.

- Achievement did not increase if more time was spent on homework.

The study went on to stress that these findings did not mean that elementary school children should not be given homework but that parents should not expect homework to affect achievement. It added that homework had three additional advantages:

1. It promotes good study habits.

2. It fosters positive attitudes towards school.

3. It makes it clear to children that learning can also take place outside school.

Research from the anti-homework lobby

Negative effects on family life

It puts too much stress on busy parents; it robs children of valuable time that could be spent developing other interests or participating in sports;

families have less time together doing things as a family – unstructured family time is shrinking in the face of longer working weeks and more hours of homework than ever before; it causes some parents ('Volvo Vigilantes'!) to demand increased homework, putting excessive pressure on their children (in the hope that this will enhance their chances of getting into the college of their choice); it interferes with what parents want to teach children; 50 per cent of parents reported having a serious family argument about homework; 34 per cent of parents reported that homework was a source of stress and struggle within the family.

The 'fatigue factor'

Older students are putting in between 50 and 60 hours per week of lesson time and homework time: consequently, they 'burn out' before they go to college; it alienates students from academic material.

Low achievers

Students with family circumstances (chaotic family lives, cramped living quarters, parents working at night) which make homework difficult mention homework as a determining factor in their decision to leave school; 20 per cent of children live in poverty and homework exacerbates their academic problems; poorer parents cannot overcome their lack of the resources and time needed to make sure their children complete school assignments.

Homework and television

A recent study has found that combining television and homework leads to an overload of information that exceeds attention capacity. Therefore, only part of the information can be processed. It made no difference whether pupils just had the sound or the picture and the sound. The major distraction was looking up at the screen, which students did on average 2.5 times per minute.

Somehow *I* managed to get my A-level revision done in front of *Thunderbirds*!

Priorities for future research
(those little grey areas)

The government have published their homework guidelines with remarkably little research under their belts. The words 'horse,' 'bolted' and 'stable door' spring to mind. The guidelines draw on what the government describes as 'current good practice', an Ofsted study carried out in 1997 and experience gained through the National Literacy and Numeracy projects.

The National Foundation for Education and Research want the following fundamental questions answered:

- Do the costs of homework at primary level outweigh the benefits for pupils, parents and teachers?

- Which kinds of homework are most effective?

- Can homework be designed so that it encourages *appropriate* parental involvement?

- Are homework planners beneficial?

- What are the relative merits of different approaches to marking?

- What kind of feedback is best?

- How much can new technology be used to facilitate homework?

- How does homework affect pupils' attitudes?

- How can homework be improved for lower-achieving pupils and pupils with special needs?

- What impact does the homework environment have?

- Which tasks suit which learning styles?

- Does homework at primary school really develop self-regulated learning?

3

The Homework Debate

Until really conclusive research is carried out there'll be no clear answers to the question of how beneficial homework actually is. I wish I could say that 'The Homework Debate' is *not* a feature of 'quality time' with my offspring. It usually arises if one of them has been given something they don't want to do. At its worst, homework puts untold stress on pupils, parents and teachers. At its best, it achieves all that it sets out to do.

Homework: the 'black hole'

Accountability

The increased focus on test scores and outcomes and the call for greater accountability has put increased pressure on a perceived need for homework.

- If we leave a sizable portion of learning to parents, how can we hold schools and teachers accountable for meeting higher standards?

- Homework is an unknown variable and standardized tests call for a tightly controlled system.

Manner of completion

- How can teachers know the level of their students' learning if they don't know how they are getting their assignments done at home?

- Did the students do their own work?

- Did they exchange answers with friends?

- Did they get an answer through e-mail or the Internet?

- Did they download the entire assignment?

Homework's threat to the learning process

- Cognitive learning's premise is that we must 'scaffold' new learning onto existing mental frameworks to build new knowledge. Understanding mistakes is a crucial part of the teaching process. Teachers cannot know exactly why a mistake has occurred if the mistake is made at home. Therefore, they cannot accurately gauge whether the student has acquired new knowledge or needs to go back to the 'scaffold' stage.

- Piaget says that asking children to perform tasks before they are developmentally ready has been proven to be counterproductive to development. Does homework fall into this category?

- Physical movement is very important in the learning process. Homework reduces time for sporting activities and, by its very nature, tends to be a sedentary occupation.

School reform on the cheap

Other, more expensive changes would increase student performance more. These are: smaller class sizes; pre-school nurseries; and increased resources for teachers.

Homework sucks!

1. Homework can be *detrimental* to *schools* because: negative attitudes are fostered; pupils don't have a chance to develop academic skills from everyday life; parents put too much pressure on their children; in explaining material in a different way, parents may confuse their children; parents may not reinforce the school's ethos with regard to learning; parents may do the work for their children or give them too much help; pupils may cheat or copy; it increases the gap between the very able and less able pupils.

2. Homework can have a *negative impact* on *families* because it: disrupts family life; causes friction within the family.

3. Homework can be *detrimental* to the *individual* when it: causes anxiety; reduces motivation; creates boredom, fatigue and emotional exhaustion; reduces time for leisure activities.

4. Homework can have a *negative effect* on *society* if: it reduces time for involvement in community activities; it polarizes children from different socio-economic circumstances because some have better facilities and resources than others.

Homework rules!

1. Homework can *promote* academic *learning* because: it increases the amount of time students spend studying; it provides opportunities for practice, preparation and extension work; it helps with the development of a range of intellectual skills.

2. Homework can *assist* the development of *generic skills* because: it provides opportunities for individualized work; it fosters initiative and independence; it develops skills in using libraries and other learning resources, such as the Internet; it trains pupils to plan and organize their time; it develops good habits and self-discipline; it encourages pupils to be responsible for their own learning.

3. Homework can *help schools* because: it gives more time for the curriculum and enables examination and coursework demands to be met; it allows assessment of pupils' progress; it enables the monitoring of pupils' understanding; it fulfils the expectations of parents, pupils, politicians and the general public; it helps with the issue of schools being accountable to external inspection agencies.

4. Homework *promotes* the *links* between *home* and *school* because: it encourages the involvement of parents; it develops links and opportunities for dialogue between parents and the school; it makes parents more knowledgeable about the school curriculum; it enables parents to become more

involved in the assessment of children's progress; it enhances esteem between parents, pupils and teachers; it underpins Home School Agreements; it establishes contact with *all* parents, irrespective of the catchment areas, because there is no reliance on parents coming into school (providing the children act as messengers).

5. Homework *promotes family communication* because: it encourages parents and children to work together; fathers become more involved in the children's education; it promotes joint family activities, creating a learning ethos in the home.

Homework: why?

The reasons for giving homework change as the child gets older. In the early stages, it is the forging of a constructive relationship between schools and home that is of primordial importance. Literacy and numeracy are given priority. Gradually, increased student autonomy and more advanced study skills become more important.

The government demands that school homework policies should set out clearly the purposes of homework. This they have done. But, for every good intention there is at least one correlating problem or disadvantage. At the risk of wantonly appearing like the devil's advocate, I shall *attempt* to illustrate this:

◆ Encouraging pupils to develop the skills, confidence and motivation needed to study effectively on their own, BUT:

- How do we know they're working on their own? Who actually did the homework?
- Not all pupils are blessed with an appropriate working environment.
- These skills should be encouraged at school where learning opportunities for *all* pupils are maximized.
- Consolidating work covered at school, BUT:
  - The level of understanding gained at school would vary enormously – would the task be appropriate for *all* pupils?
  - Do we really know whose level of understanding would be assessed?
- Developing self-discipline, BUT:
  - Some pupils don't get the support required.
  - They've been cooped up all day in a classroom – give them a break!
  - Is the task meaningful and relevant or just something that promotes self-discipline?
- Improving research skills, BUT:
  - By pursuing their *out-of-school* interests, research skills could be developed just as effectively.
- Promoting the pupil/parent/teacher partnership, BUT:
  - Homework can achieve the exact opposite.
  - There are other ways of fostering and nurturing these relationships.
- Managing particular demands, such as GCSE coursework, BUT:
  - The very nature of coursework completed at home means that one can't be absolutely certain *who* did the work.

Homework

- Some pupils have access to more resources than others.
- Coursework overburdens all concerned and should not be a homework issue.

The debate will undoubtedly rage on. In any case, we have to follow the government guidelines, so we can stick any objections we may have into our pipes and smoke them.

4

Government Guidelines for Homework

General points:

- Schools should have a written school *homework policy* that is led by the senior management of the school as part of the school's overall learning and assessment strategy. It should be accessible to pupils, parents and teachers; clearly understood by teachers, pupils and parents; regularly monitored and reviewed in consultation with *all* parties. The timing and manner (checking of homework diaries and assignments, discussion with subject teachers/pupils/parents, staff appraisal, surveys) must be made clear. The framework for more detailed guidance should be drawn up by subject faculties and departments; conducive to the setting of appropriate tasks (age, ability and other relevant factors), creating a balanced and manageable programme for pupils and teachers alike; mindful of the fact that the purposes of homework change as the child gets older. There should also be information about study opportunities within and outside the school.

- Homework arrangements must be manageable for *everyone* as well as being educationally beneficial.

27

Homework

- Homework should not get in the way of other after-school activities like sport, music and clubs.

- A wide range of after-school activities will be made available to pupils who have not had access to them in the past.

- Pupils should have frequent and increasing opportunities to develop and consolidate their competence as independent learners, through: homework diaries and planners; tutorials on study skills; target setting; mentoring schemes.

- There are no guidelines specifically for special schools because of the range of ages and abilities. They should adopt aspects of primary and secondary guidelines that are relevant to them.

The amount of homework

The *intrinsic value* of homework activities is far more important than the amount given. Policies should contain clear and flexible guidance as to the amount of homework expected of pupils of different ages:

- Years 1-2: 1 hour per week

- Years 3-4: 1.5 hours per week

- Year 5: 30 minutes per day

- Year 6: 30 minutes per day

- Years 7-8: 45-90 minutes per day

- Year 9: 1-2 hours per day

- Years 10-11: 1.5-2.5 hours per day

◆ Years 12–13: depending on pupils individual programme, guidance should be included in school policies.

Planning and coordination

◆ In order to ensure consistency and progression: assignments could be planned along with the scheme of work; a bank of tasks could be created, ensuring flexibility as well as progression.

◆ National and local support services on the Internet can prove to be invaluable resources for planning.

◆ Homework timetables must be coordinated across the subjects, indicating time allocations for each day.

◆ It is recommended that teachers and pupils are issued with homework diaries to help implement and monitor the homework timetable.

◆ Pupils having difficulties meeting homework deadlines should not be excused homework, but given extra help with strategies to manage it.

◆ Homework arrangements, including sanctions for non-completion of tasks, should be applied consistently across the school so that the system is seen to be fair.

◆ Homework must be set, managed and marked consistently across the school.

◆ Pupils must receive prompt, clear feedback on their work.

Parents and carers

Parents and carers must:

- Be told what they are expected to do to support children with their homework and how their roles will change as the pupil moves up the school.

- Provide a peaceful, suitable place in which pupils can do their homework, or

- Help pupils attend other places where homework can be done, such as homework clubs or study support centres.

- Make the importance of homework clear to their children.

- Encourage and praise children when homework is done.

- Ensure that deadlines are met.

Homework and study support facilities

- The government plans to provide lottery money to support out-of-school learning, which will eventually be available in all schools.

- LEAs with Premier or Division 1 football clubs will be given funding to establish study centres at the clubs, offering support on: literacy; numeracy; IT; homework. Details of these should be included in the school policy.

- Homework policies should encourage the use of

study support facilities where appropriate, both in and out of the school setting.

The implementation of guidelines: primary schools

Stating your purpose in giving homework

The government's reasons for giving homework have already been made explicit. Whatever reasons your policy states, you and your school need to make sure that your stated purpose requires:

- Consistency of approach throughout the school.
- Progression towards independence and individual responsibility.
- The needs of the individual pupil to be taken into account.
- The clear understanding of parents and guardians of what is expected of them.
- The improvement of the pupils' learning experience.
- The facilitation of reinforcement and revision.
- Strengthening of the relationship between parents, pupils and school.
- Increased collaboration between parent and child with regard to the child's learning.
- Opportunity to talk to an interested adult about what they are learning.

Homework

- Practice in key skills in a supportive environment.

- Development of long-term strategies for future needs.

- The children being prepared for secondary school. (Primary schools that form part of local pyramids or clusters should co-ordinate their policies.)

All of the above purposes of homework apply equally to pupils with special educational needs. Most importantly, homework should *not* be seen as a way of helping them to catch up with their peers. The policy must make this explicit.

Homework: what type?

Policies must give clear guidance about the sort of homework to be given. At primary school, the main focuses should be literacy and numeracy. Other subjects can be introduced gradually, but the emphasis must remain on these two areas.

Activities might include: formal, traditional written exercises; joint activities with parents or carers; reading; listening to others read; learning spellings; practising pronunciation; number games; finding out information; preparing oral presentations.

The needs of pupils with special educational needs will vary from individual to individual and from school to school. School policies must state that, for SEN pupils, homework must: strike an appropriate balance between setting differentiated special tasks and following the mainstream curriculum; have a very clear focus and time guideline; give plenty of opportunities for pupils to succeed; help develop social as well as other skills; be varied and not purely written assignments; be manageable for teachers.

Scheduling of homework

It's one thing having a piece of paper that states what and how much homework should be done; it's quite another making sure that what is given is manageable. Therefore, it is absolutely essential that the policy clearly states who is responsible for ensuring that the demands of homework are:

- ◆ Reasonable for pupils, parents and carers (normally the class teacher).

- ◆ Manageable for teachers (usually a member of the senior management team).

- ◆ Well coordinated and structured, especially with regard to literacy and numeracy.

The implementation of guidelines: secondary schools

The purpose, type and scheduling of homework must be seen to continue the good work of the primary school. Therefore, the implementation of these aspects of homework will be much the same. When implementing your school policy make sure the following points are taken into consideration:

- ◆ During the secondary phase, the emphasis gradually shifts from home–school liaison to increased pupil autonomy.

33

Homework

♦ The primordial importance of literacy and numeracy shifts towards a much broader range of subjects.

A sample homework policy: primary

Policies can be directed at any of the parties concerned – pupils, teachers, parents, or all three. The following example is directed at the pupils.

St. Trinian's Primary School: Homework Policy

Here are some of the reasons why we think **homework is important**:

♦ It gives you responsibility and helps you to learn on your own.
♦ It helps your parents get to know what you are doing in school. Then, they can help in all sorts of other ways, like taking you to visit places or watching and recording television programmes with you.
♦ It gives you the chance to do things at home which are difficult at school.
♦ It means you can be helped on your own with things you find hard.
♦ You can practise spelling and times tables and get better at them.

Everyone can get **help**.
Not everyone has people who have time to work with and help him or her. It is important that homework is fair for everyone. Here are the times and places for getting help if you need it:

Government Guidelines for Homework

Library: Monday and Wednesday lunchtimes.
You can get help from:

+ Year 6 pupils.
+ The librarians.

They can help with:

+ Reading.
+ Writing.
+ Spelling.
+ Maths games and puzzles.

Anyone who hasn't been able to do their homework can come.

Library: Mondays after school.
You can get help from:

+ Some parents.
+ A teacher.

You can get individual help with:

+ Any homework problems.

Anyone from Years 3, 4, 5 or 6 can come.

What **sort** of homework will you get?

+ Reading to others or reading by yourself.
+ Talking about what you have read:
  + The people in the book.
  + What has happened in the book.
  + What you think is going to happen next.
+ Practising your tables.
+ Counting in different intervals.
+ Learning spelling.
+ Doing investigations.

Homework

- Collecting data.
- Doing experiments.

You will not often be asked to finish work off as this is not fair for people who work slowly or find the work hard.

How long will it take to do your homework?
Reception and Year 1

- **Ten minutes** reading with a parent, carer or member of Year 6.
- **Ten minutes** playing word or number games.
- You may be asked to make something, collect data or find information. This may take more than ten minutes but you will have fun.
- Your homework will be written in your diary by your teacher.

Year 2

- You will get **15–20 minutes** of homework each day.
- You will do the same sorts of homework as in Year 1.
- You will have some practical investigations to do.
- You may have to collect data or information by measuring, counting or asking people questions.
- Your teacher will write your homework in your diary or ask you to do it.

Years 3, 4, 5 and 6

- Years 3 and 4 will have **20 minutes** of homework each day.
- Years 5 and 6 will have **30 minutes** each day.
- You will be given the work on Mondays, Wednesdays and Fridays.
- You may be asked to:
  - Practise tables.
  - Practise counting in different ways.

- Learn spellings.
- Read fiction or non-fiction books.
- Discuss what you have read with your parents, carers or at homework club.
- Do investigations, collect data or interview people. You may need help from your family.
- Practise skills such as measuring or weighing to find information.
- *Occasionally* finish work from school.

You must write this down in your diaries.

A sample homework policy: secondary

The following example is directed at pupils, parents and teachers.

Grange Hill Comprehensive School: Homework Policy

The Purpose of Homework

- To encourage pupils to develop the skills, confidence and motivation needed to study effectively on their own. This is vital, given the future importance for pupils of lifelong learning and adaptability.
- Consolidating and reinforcing skills and understanding developed at school.
- Extending school learning, for example through additional reading.
- Sustaining the involvement of parents and carers in the management of pupils' learning and keeping them informed about the work the pupils are doing.

Homework

- Managing particular demands, such as GCSE course-work.

How Homework is Organized

- The homework timetable shows which subjects are set each night.
- The pupils are expected to spend the following amounts of time on their homework:
  - Year 7: 30–60 minutes.
  - Year 8: 30–70 minutes.
  - Year 9: 30–80 minutes.
  - Year 10: 60–110 minutes.
  - Year 11: 60–110 minutes.
- Pupils are given a journal in which to record all homework tasks.

The Responsibilities of the Pupil

Pupils are expected to:

- Always write down a summary of their homework in their homework journal.
- Always have their journal with them and get it signed at home by a parent/carer every week.
- Complete homework to the best of their ability within the appropriate length of time.
- Submit homework at the time requested.

It is recommended that pupils get into the habit of doing homework on the night it is set and designating a regular homework time.

The Responsibilities of Parents/Carers

Parents/carers are expected to:

- Provide a reasonably peaceful, suitable place in which pupils can do homework.
- Make it clear to pupils that they value homework and

Government Guidelines for Homework

support the school in explaining how homework can help them make progress at school.
- Encourage and praise pupils when they have completed homework.
- Expect deadlines to be met and check that they are.
- Sign the homework journal once a week.

The Responsibilities of the Teacher

Teachers are expected to:

- Set homework of appropriate duration at the time specified in the homework timetable.
- Set tasks that provide a suitable challenge for all pupils.
- Allow more than 24 hours for the completion of homework tasks.
- Avoid setting homework in the final few minutes of the lesson.
- Avoid the regular setting of 'finish class work' as a homework task.
- Monitor the completion of homework by pupils. Failure to complete homework will result in the following hierarchy of punishments: 1st offence: reprimand; 2nd offence: detention; 3rd offence: parents informed.

Teachers are *not* expected to:

- Mark every piece of homework.
- Always set formal written tasks.

Teachers may set a variety of tasks: investigations; research; reading; drawing; interviews; designing; word processing; simple experiments; drafting; revision; desktop publishing; essay writing; report writing; model making; coursework.

Homework

The Responsibilities of the Head of Department

Heads of department are expected to:

- Lead their teams in discussing and developing homework tasks.
- Monitor the setting of homework by all members of their team.
- Monitor the quality and appropriateness of homework set by their team.

The Responsibilities of the Head of Year

Heads of year are expected to:

- Support members of their team in inspecting and initialling homework journals.
- Monitor this process within their teams.

The Responsibilities of the Tutor

Tutors are expected to:

- Ensure that the members of their tutor groups understand the homework timetable and how the school expects the homework journal to be organized.
- Ensure that at the start of every term all members of their tutor groups write in homework subjects in their journals on the appropriate night.
- Monitor the completion of the homework journal by their pupils and initial them at least twice every half term.
- Be aware if any pupil has home circumstances that make the completion of homework difficult and encourage such pupils to work after school in the library.

5

Homework Policies and the Teacher

You are accountable! Gone are the days when teachers just did their own thing and hoped for the best. When trouble arises, whether it's a disgruntled pupil, parent or school manager, the buck stops with *you*. A horrified school inspector will look to *you* first, if your homework strategies are not up to scratch. Look at yourself first: do *all* your homework tasks conform to your school's policy and/or government guidelines?

BUT: don't shoulder all of the responsibility. It is up to an appropriate member of the school management team to ensure that you're getting enough support from 'above'. If you're not, it's *their* responsibility. To help you assess whether you're doing things correctly and whether your school's management is enabling you to do your job, here are a set of questions to ask yourself:

- How does your school define homework?
- Does your school have a homework policy?
- Have you seen it?
- Were you involved in formulating this policy?
- Is your role with regard to homework clearly defined?

Homework

- Do you have access to year group guidelines?

- Are there regular reviews and updates of your school's policy?

- Are you involved in any discussions regarding modifications to the homework policy?

- Has your school's purpose in giving homework been made clear to you?

- Is your homework an *integral* part of your programme of learning?

- Do you plan your homework *creatively*?

- Do you *plan* your homework as carefully as you plan your lessons?

- Do you take account of the *range* of pupils' abilities?

- If necessary, do you draw on appropriate expertise, such as subject and SEN specialists?

- When you give *differentiated* tasks, is this based on *prior assessment*?

- Do your tasks provide an *equal* and *appropriate* challenge for individuals?

- Was your homework planned to *complement* rather than complete classroom *learning*?

- Did you have the opportunity to plan and prepare tasks and materials as a member of a team, or were you left to do it on your own?

- Did the time you spent preparing homework

materials mean that you could make more *effective* use of *teaching time*?

- Did the school provide you with a homework planner to make achieving all of the above manageable? Do you use it?

- Does your school stress the *importance* of homework to the *pupils*?

- Does your school *actively encourage parents* to support their children with regard to homework?

- Do parents understand *why* you need their assistance?

- Have parents been reassured that *no specialist knowledge* is required?

- Do you make a point of placing *equal* value on the contributions of *all* parents?

- Do you make sure you don't put *too many demands* on parents?

- Do you regularly *thank* parents for their support?

- Are you *well-informed* about the *family circumstances* of *all* your pupils?

- Do you take particular care to liaise with parents of children with *special needs* to ensure that tasks are appropriate and feasible?

- Does your school have clear and consistent strategies for assessing performance? Do you know what they are?

Homework

- Do you set homework in accordance with individual learning programmes?

- Do you enhance progression through feedback on homework performance?

- Does your feedback show the pupil what and how to improve?

- Do you always acknowledge and praise homework that is completed well?

- Do you tell the pupils the criteria used when work is assessed?

- Do you expect high standards for homework assignments?

- Is there progression in your homework tasks? Does time allocation increase?

- Do the type and level of study skills required demand progress?

- Are you given time to plan homework?

- Do you have marking time?

- Do you have adequate resources?

- Do you have access to facilities for preparing banks of homework?

- Does your homework reflect developments within education and the range of learning styles (such as ICT and 'Accelerated Learning')?

- Does your school have a homework schedule or timetable of subjects and tasks for all year groups?

- Does your school consistently make sure that pupils comply with the schedule?

- Do all other members of staff follow the schedule? If not, is there someone responsible for ensuring they do?

- Does your school have rewards and sanctions attached to their homework policy? Are they clearly defined? Do all staff apply them consistently?

- Are your pupils and their parents aware of online educational resources?

- If pupils don't have the Internet at home, have they been made aware of how to gain access to a computer?

- Are pupils regularly warned about safety on the Internet?

6

A Checklist for School Managers

If staff can answer 'yes' to all the questions in Chapter 5, then off you go to get your Nobel Prize for services to homework! Here's a list just to make sure you'll be in the running.

- Does your school have a homework strategy?

- Is your homework strategy actively and regularly evaluated?

- Do you develop your homework strategy with an eye to future needs?

- Is homework an integral part of your school's plan for learning?

- Does your homework strategy meet the needs of your particular school?

- Does your homework strategy fit in with the school's goals?

- Could your homework strategy be readily developed to meet existing goals more effectively?

- Could your homework strategy be modified to address new priorities?

- Do you involve teachers, parents and pupils in the process of formulating and modifying your school's policy?

A Checklist for School Managers

- Have you clearly defined the roles of teachers, pupils and parents with regard to homework?

- Do you use a variety of channels and media to keep parents and pupils informed about homework?

- Do you encourage parents and pupils to share responsibility for the pupils' learning?

- Have you issued guidelines for each year group?

- Do you issue regular class/subject newsletters?

- Do the pupils have homework planners or diaries?

- Have teachers been made aware of the school's definition of homework?

- Have the teachers reached a broad consensus with regard to the purpose of homework?

- Have you specified a range of homework tasks appropriate to each year group, making special provisions for SEN pupils?

- Do you ensure that differentiated homework is appropriate?

- Do you allow curriculum time for teachers to plan and prepare homework tasks and materials?

- Do you give teachers the opportunity to plan and prepare tasks and resources as a team?

- Do you make sure staff are well informed about family circumstances?

- What strategies do you use to involve parents in their children's learning?

Homework

- How do you collaborate with parents of children with special needs?

- What alternative opportunities (such as individual help, the use of IT and homework clubs) are provided?

- What study support initiatives are available in your area? Are all parties aware of them and encouraged to use them?

- Do you ensure that assessment and feedback is consistent across all curricular areas?

- Do you regularly check feedback given to children to ensure that it complies with policy guidelines?

- Do you make certain that homework programmes plan for progression with regard to time allocation, type and level of study skills required?

- Do you ensure staff have curriculum time for preparation and marking?

- Do teachers and pupils have access to appropriate resources, such as textbooks and other published material?

- Do you make sure there are facilities provided for staff to prepare banks of homework resources or tasks?

- Is the homework programme clearly and consistently implemented?

- Do your homework guidelines include a timetable which includes when, how often and due dates for homework tasks?

A Checklist for School Managers

- Do you regularly monitor that staff comply with the homework timetable?

- If you have a rewards and sanctions system, how do you ensure that it's clearly defined and consistently applied?

- Do you regularly monitor the effectiveness of your homework policy, involving teachers, pupils and parents?

- Are teachers, pupils and parents regularly informed of resources available on the Internet?

- If pupils don't have access to computers in the home, how do you ensure they have access to one in school?

- Do you inform pupils about ICT facilities outside school (such as libraries and Internet cafes)?

- Do you warn pupils and parents of the dangers of the Internet on an ongoing basis?

- Do you actively campaign for study support initiatives in your area? Do you encourage teachers, pupils and parents to do the same?

7

Homework and the Internet

Platitude coming up: the Internet is an *invaluable* source of information. Many encyclopaedias are now online. The National Curriculum has an extensive online site with links for pupils, teachers and parents. Also, there are sites specifically created, many of them by teachers, to assist with homework problems. These are searchable homework sites with live questions and answers. Many of them have extensive libraries. You and the school should furnish pupils and parents with a list of recommended sites. Here are some examples:

- *All Experts   www.allexperts.com*
  The oldest and largest free question-and-answer site.

- *AS Guru   www.bbc.co.uk/education/asguru*
  Revision for A level.

- *Bitesize   www.bbc.co.uk/schools/gcsebitesize*
  This assists with revision for Key Stage 3 and GCSE.

- *Homework High   www.homeworkhigh.com*
  Channel 4's site aims to help with just about any question you can throw at them! There's a library of 35,000 questions and answers. If you can't find

what you're looking for, you can submit your own questions.

- *Kevin's Playroom   www.kevinsplayroom.co.uk*
  This is a unique multi-award winning website produced by children for children. It lists all school subjects with approved links to curriculum-based information. This site is aimed at children from pre-school through to secondary level to assist with all aspects of schoolwork.

- *Science Line   www.sciencenet.org.uk*
  Science Line's website offers a database of answers based around the questions received by their free phone question helpline. This is the UK's only free national science information service. You can speak to a scientist and find out the answer to any tricky questions (0800 800 4000).

- *SOS Teacher www.bbc.co.uk/schools/sosteacher*
  More homework help from the BBC.

Subject teachers may wish to issue lists of recommended sites for their own curricular area.

As a fantastic homework aid, the Internet brings an incredible amount of knowledge to pupils' fingertips. Pupils should be encouraged to be disciplined and effective when surfing for study. Pupils and parents must be made aware of the pitfalls of Internet research:

1. Intellectual theft – pupils have no control over who accesses their work and what is then done to it. Also, they may inadvertently steal someone else's work, breaching copyright laws.

Homework

2. Time wasting – this can make research a lengthy process.

3. Credibility of the information they receive – they need to be told that material is not guaranteed to be accurate and, in some cases, is risibly inaccurate.

Here is some advice that could be given to parents and pupils:

◆ Parents should try to get involved in work that requires use of the Internet.

◆ Encourage children to be selective, rather than indiscriminate about the information they receive.

◆ Make sure that the information given on the site is aimed at the child's age group.

◆ If there is no sign of the author's or publisher's name, there is no guarantee that the information is legitimate.

◆ Check that the links to any website are well respected. Reputable websites will not touch dodgy ones with a barge pole.

◆ Check the ownership of the website and make sure that it is educational rather than commercial or serving the interests of hate-motivated groups. There's a site called *Who Is* that can help you to trace the ownership and affiliations of websites.

◆ Pupils should be encouraged to use more than one source of information in order to avoid bias.

◆ Parents and pupils must be aware that if they

don't source material they use, they could be guilty of plagiarism or intellectual theft.

There are other, more obvious dangers associated with the Internet. Parents may need to be advised about dealing with the following:

◆ Pornography: filtering software; keeping a log of children's Internet activity; checking discs regularly for inappropriate content.

◆ Paedophiles: banning chatrooms; allowing educational chatrooms but supervising use (*Grid Club Chat* offers safe places where children can chat to other grid members).

◆ E-mail: filter software recognizes and stops certain word phrases and attachments.

◆ Privacy issues: children should never post a named photo of themselves on the web.

Here are a few safety sites that help with the above:

◆ *BBC Chat Guide* An easy-to-understand site with a common-sense guide to using chat rooms for the whole family.

◆ *Internet Watch Foundation* This site is full of advice and you can report unsuitable activity on the Internet.

◆ *Childnet International* Gives very valuable information on how to discuss Internet safety with children. Useful for parents and teachers alike.

◆ *Be Safe Online* A site that informs adults about the dangers of the Internet so that they can

Homework

encourage safe use by children and young people.

- *Kidsmart* A site for teachers, families and children. Has resources, games and activities to encourage web safety.

- *BrowserLock* Gives access to a list of approved websites. The list can be added to by the supervisor.

- *Net Nanny* Invisibly monitors Internet use, screening out words and content determined by the parent or administrator.

- *We-Blocker* A site that blocks out or allows material for individual members of the family. Therefore, adults can still have access to adult material on the same computer.

- *Wise Up to the Net* The Home Office's safety advice for parents.

8

The Pupils' Perspective

They are tired, they've been working all day, they'd rather do something else. In their position, would you be naturally inclined to take on and relish even more work at the end of the day? Every pupil, however diligent, will feel like this at some stage when it comes to homework. Strategies for motivating pupils will be dealt with in a later chapter. There aren't many young people who'll publicly say that they really loved the homework and could they possibly have more of the same! More usual is the grumbling and agonized moaning when you generously bestow a homework task on the writhing masses. Sometimes these complaints can be taken at face value. Occasionally, however, there may be a hidden message.

'This is boring.'

Try to resist the temptation to beat them about the head with a wet fish. This excruciatingly irritating utterance could really mean: 'I don't understand.'

'It's far too much!'

Ask yourself if the work is interesting enough. Pupils who are enjoying their work will be happy to work much harder than those who aren't. It might be their way of saying: 'I'd rather watch paint dry.'

'I'm not doing it!'

It may not be a matter of blatant defiance. Ask yourself if the pupil lacks confidence in his ability to do the task. Do you think he understands the task? Have you clearly indicated the relevance of the homework? It may really mean: 'I *can't* do this!/ I doubt I'll be able to do it/ What's the point of this?'

'I hate writing.'

Writing is a permanent record. There's more risk involved. If a mistake is made, it's there for everyone to see. This may mean: 'I'm afraid I may be (seen to be) wrong.'

'I hate reading.'

Is the pupil a confident reader? This might really be a case of: 'I'm embarrassed because my reading's not too hot.'

Feedback and monitoring of homework need to be handled carefully, too. A lack of homework must be chased up. Even if they may feel smug that they've got away with it, they will also think you don't care. If you make exceptions of pupils who you believe are disadvantaged in some way, they may not perceive this as kind, even if, overtly, they appear grateful. They may think you think they'll fail anyway so there's no point in chasing them up. Writing copious comments on their work may not be seen as a sign of your deep concern that they progress. However positive you may try to be, too much scrawl, red or otherwise, may be perceived as you tearing their work apart. Conversely, trite, repetitive remarks may be received as a sign that you're in 'auto-tick' mode and couldn't give a monkey's what they've written. Pupils who are constantly asking for their mark are not necessarily casting aspersions on your efficacy as a teacher. Don't be tempted to shower them with a torrent of invective. It may be an unprecedented sign that they've put a lot of effort into the work.

9

Homework and the Parent

No homework policy will work without the support of a parent. Most policies will indicate how and why parents should help. Many parents will know what they can do. However, you may need to make it more explicit to others, whose own experience of homework was, at worst, non-existent, and at best, haphazard.

Information to give to parents

How much homework?

- Their child should not be spending significantly longer on homework than set out in your policy's guidelines. Is this happening? Why?

- The time allocations are guidelines – providing the task is completed, it doesn't matter if it doesn't take as long.

- The amount of homework should be spread evenly throughout the week.

What type of homework?

- All homework activities should be related to work children are doing at school.

- Homework will not always be written work. It may include: reading; informal games to practise mathematical skills; preparing a presentation; finding out information; making something; trying a simple scientific experiment; cooking.

How much help?

- Schools are keen for parents to support and help children.

- There are times when teachers want to see what the children can do on their own.

- Coursework can be supervised by parents but not completed by them (stress that this would be in breach of examination regulations).

Where to do homework?

At home

- Does the child have a quiet space with a table or desk?

- Can younger children be kept out of their way?

At a study support centre

Over the next few years, many schools will be given funding so they can provide study support for children out of school hours. Study support will be available in other centres too.

Homework

- Are parents aware of what the Study Support Initiative aims to achieve?

- What is or will be available in your area? Do your parents and pupils know?

Feedback?

Parents should be aware of feedback given to children. Make sure that they know why, when and how feedback will be given. All feedback should involve a comment on what the child did well, and how he can improve.

10 pieces of advice to give to parents

1. Use praise and encouragement to boost their child's confidence.

2. Read to and with their child as much as possible.

3. Encourage their child to observe and talk about his surroundings.

4. Make use of the local library.

5. Visit museums and places their child might find interesting.

6. Watch television with their child and talk about it afterwards.

7. Set aside a regular time for homework.

8. Give their child space and peace to do his work.

9. Discuss homework, including any feedback.
10. Point out the interesting and enjoyable aspects of homework.

How to Vary your Homework Tasks

The very nature of most homework policies is that homework will be set regularly. This is beneficial in that the pupil will find is easier to organize his time. However, unless tasks are varied, homework will quickly seem like meaningless drudgery – for teachers as well as pupils. Teachers in all subject areas should be aware of different learning styles and activities that acknowledge how individual pupils best learn.

There are eight main learning styles:

1. **Linguistic**: reading; essay writing; producing a report; learning a poem; preparing a speech; interviewing; drafting.

2. **Mathematical/Logical:** problem solving; research; investigations; simple experiments; projects; interpreting data; designing.

3. **Bodily/Kinaesthetic:** making a model; practising a dance; play rehearsal; practising a P.E. skill; exercise.

4. **Visual:** drawing; report writing; designing; graphicacy.

5. **Musical:** listening to music; composing; reading music; learning a song in a foreign language; practising a musical instrument; making a musical instrument.

6. Intrapersonal: reflecting; producing a diary; writing a personal story.

7. Interpersonal: visiting a local library; interviewing; undertaking a community project; preparing a debate; preparing an assembly.

8. Naturalist: finding out more about nature and the natural world around us; undertaking an environmental project; research into the environment; visiting a local city farm; an investigation into a local issue.

DO NOT:

- Assign homework as a punishment.

- Use it to complete whatever you couldn't do in class.

- Use it to introduce students to complicated subject matter.

- Customize assignments for every student – the pay-offs are not that large and not worth the bother.

11

Motivating Reluctant Pupils

Every pupil is different and will be motivated by different factors. Some will only need to know that the homework policy is consistent and fair and that homework is unavoidable. Others will benefit from a system of rewards and sanctions. The naturally competitive spirit of most human beings can also be harnessed to suit the homework arena! Listen to your pupils – they will often let you know what motivates them.

If it's appropriate, occasionally you might ask them to design their own homework task. The only remit is that it has to be homework that makes them think.

In addition to the homework, ask them to write a paragraph or so, describing what they did and what they learned from it. You can follow the tasks up by asking pupils to share their work with the rest of the class, either by giving a presentation or displaying their work on the classroom wall.

They can design the homework for themselves to do or for others in the class. Most would relish the opportunity. They may also particularly love to set their teacher a task. Tell them you'll choose the five best ones and they can vote on which one you do.

Actively demand their feedback:

◆ Was there anything they didn't understand?

- Did they have trouble getting the necessary books and materials?

- How could a task be changed to make it more interesting?

They'll appreciate that you are prepared to listen to their views and are not merely a homework-spewing robot on a mission.

Sometimes, you could give the students a choice between two pieces of homework. The feeling of empowerment will motivate some of them. Transforming homework into a matter of choice as opposed to obligation can be highly rewarding for all concerned. By giving students choice, you are offering them trust, freedom and responsibility. Everyone appreciates that! Use these choice-giving assignments sparingly. Otherwise, the students will run out of inspiration and the whole thing will fall flat.

Ensure that your approach to homework is consistent and fair. In this way you can create an environment in which your pupils are comfortable with the idea of doing their homework. Rewards, sanctions and competitions will only work if you have a solid foundation in your approach to homework. Ask yourself the following key questions:

1. *Have I laid out my expectations early in the year?* Make sure everyone realizes that homework is important and has meaning; stress that not completing homework will have consequences; state when and how much homework will be given; tell them you expect high standards; explain that parents will be asked to be closely

involved in the homework process; give explicit examples of what is acceptable and what is not (for example: readability; presentation; completeness; attention to detail; explanation of answers; neatness of graphs/drawings; adherence to due dates).

2. *Have I created assignments that have a purpose?*
Purposes include: they review and practise what has been learned in class; they prepare for the next class; they help pupils to learn to use resources, such as libraries, reference materials and the Internet; they explore subjects more fully than time permits in class; they teach students to work independently; they encourage self-discipline and responsibility; they give pupils the opportunity to practise working to deadlines.

3. *Do I always make sure the students understand the purpose of the task?*
Tell them why the assignment is important – they may not intuitively know.

4. *Are my assignments focused and clear?*
Try not to give homework just before the end of the lesson. In the manner of Pavlov's dogs, on hearing the word 'Homework', pupils will think 'Ooh, we're going soon'. They'll start thinking about that rather than listening to and understanding your instructions. Make sure your instructions are easy to follow; don't introduce or reinforce too many ideas in any given assignment.

5. *Do the tasks challenge the pupils to think or could they do it on auto-pilot?*
    Do they challenge pupils to break free from their usual way of thinking? Do they encourage a new approach to learning?

6. *Are my homework tasks varied?*
    Students quickly tire of similar assignments – mix approaches and styles. This will increase the chances that, at some stage, all students will have something they enjoy. Use long-term and short-term tasks; try to cover material that reviews and reinforces skills students have learned earlier – not just the work done that day.

7. *Do the activities I have given make learning personal?*
    Assign tasks that draw on the pupils': family; culture; community; interests.

8. *Can my tasks be seen to be relevant to the here and now of the third millennium?*
    Discuss the similarities between the present and the past; make comparisons between now and then; put a modern slant (radio or television report) on a historical event.

9. *Does the homework correspond to the skills, interests and needs of the pupils?*
    Are the tasks too easy? Are the tasks too hard? Do they match a child's preferred learning style as often as possible? Do they allow pupils to work on material they truly enjoy? Do assignments vary in style format and content to suit as many pupils as possible?

Homework

10. *Do I often make use of school and community resources?*

11. *Do the assignments tie in with my teaching style?*
Can this be seen as an extension of how I taught in class? Can the pupils see that this is a task they are doing for me personally?

12. *Is the amount of homework appropriate?*
A common mistake is unwittingly to set too much. Parents sometimes demand too much homework – resist them. Make sure all the tasks are necessary and not just repetition of a concept already mastered; check regularly with other teachers who set work on the same night as you and make sure you're not overburdening the students; watch your pupils in class and take note of how long it takes them to complete work.

13. *Do I encourage and teach good study habits?*
Are children encouraged to reliably bring work home, complete it and return it to school? Are children advised to set aside a regular time to study that fits in with other commitments? Do you tell pupils to remove distractions such as the television and telephone during homework time? Do they always have the appropriate equipment with them for completion of homework? Do they methodically record their assignments in a homework book? Are they given plenty of practice in note-taking? Are they shown how to manage their time? Do you teach them how to prepare for a test?

14. Is my feedback consistent and constructive?
Make sure you tell them where they did well and where they can improve; consistent feedback reinforces the importance of homework; only grade where it is beneficial and motivating. Use peer feedback – it benefits by: providing another perspective of their work; helping to develop co-operative skills; promoting the discussion of problems.

15. Do I give praise and motivate often enough?
Give praise often – it motivates; make sure your praise is genuine – if not, they'll see straight through it; use rewards if you think it appropriate; display outstanding work; competitions can be motivating.

16. Can pupils easily come to me for help?
Do everything to make sure you are seen as approachable so pupils are comfortable to come to you for help; schedule times to be available and make sure they are regularly reminded of them; inform students of other sources of help, such as librarians, study support centres and the Internet.

17. Would more effective communication with parents enable a higher homework completion rate?
Contact parents routinely at the beginning of the academic year, *before* problems arise; make sure they know that you are available to discuss any aspect of their child's education; make a special effort with parents who don't initiate contact;

make sure parents know how they can contact you; tell parents about homework problems as soon as they arise; ensure parents know how you want them to be involved with homework.

18. *Do I respect individual students and make sure they know it?*
Pupils will be more inclined to complete homework if there is mutual respect; instinctively, children know when teachers care about them and want them to do their best work.

19. *Make homework count!*
Make sure students know that non-completion of homework *will* effect their grading; rewards and sanctions.

Rewards and sanctions

Only when you have addressed most, if not all, of the above issues can you think about rewards and sanctions. Many schools have a rewards and sanctions system as an integral part of their homework policy. You'll probably be duty-bound to adhere to the school system, depending on how prescriptive the school managers are. As a general rule, the best strategy to adopt is to use rewards as often as possible and sanctions as infrequently as possible. Your relationship with the pupils will be vastly improved if you can create and sustain a positive ambiance in your classroom. You'll get much more out of your charges. Anything positive, embrace it wholeheartedly! But don't issue rewards unless they have truly been deserved. Make sure that any reward given is seen as a reward, rather than a patronizing pat on the head.

Only impose a sanction if you are definitely going to follow it through. Some pupils may not see your sanction as any punishment whatsoever. For example, some pupils may regard being kept in during break time on a cold winter's day as the ultimate luxury.

Some teachers give 'homework passes' as a reward for successful completion of tasks. Surely, this goes against the idea of fostering a positive attitude towards homework. Others give homework as a sanction, which, again, probably contravenes the school homework strategy.

Depending on your school, you may have a certain freedom to create your own rewards within your classroom. Also, do things with which you feel comfortable – basically, anything that creates a fun, positive atmosphere in your classroom. You might think about: promising them a game during a lesson; giving sweets, stickers or small gifts; offering to teach them in a funny wig or on roller blades; telling them a funny story; telling them an embarrassing secret; allowing them to set you a homework task; giving them a 'bonus' question that is fun or light-hearted as the end of an assignment and reading any particularly funny ones out when giving feedback. Once you get to know a class, you'll know exactly what 'floats their boat.'

Minimizing workload

With classes of 30 pupils or more, who are receiving homework twice a week, a teacher's job can be never ending.

Preparation

Provided your school has invested some time on the implementation of their homework policy, there will either already be banks of homework tasks from which you can draw, or they will already be a cohesive part of your schemes of work and lesson plans. If this is not the case, then you should be allowed non-contact time to prepare tasks and materials, either alone or with a team of colleagues. If you're on your own and building up from scratch, keep it simple. In your enthusiasm, try not to get carried away inventing complicated motivational games and activities that involve a great deal of preparation.

Setting the task

If you insist on setting written tasks for every homework, then very soon you'll have no time for anything else and the men in the white coats may have to come and take you away. When planning lessons, bear in mind the marking workload that will arise from any homework given. A teacher's job is *never* done – so, give yourself a break!

There is an almost infinite number of alternatives to written assignments. Some of these have been dealt with in a previous chapter. Such tasks can be thought up and given in no time at all. Often, these are enjoyed more by the pupils as well, and that's half the battle. Another bonus is that there's no marking, saving your sanity and, possibly, a great deal of red ink!

Marking and feedback

If you give tasks that don't require marking, then you have significantly reduced your workload. Feedback is often verbal and instant. Pupils do rate their teachers on how quickly they return work. Set tasks that lend themselves well to a rapid turnaround whenever you can. When collecting homework, tick off the pupils' names one by one. This will give a strong message of your serious intent, and avoids the otherwise inevitable: 'I gave it to you, Sir!'

However, written assignments must be given fairly regularly and will need to be marked. This doesn't mean you have to face the end of the day with 120 unmarked books and a deep desire to emigrate. Here are some suggestions as to how to reduce marking:

- Don't set lengthy written work unless it is absolutely necessary.

- You don't have to correct all mistakes – just indicate where the error has occurred and set corrections as the pupils' next task.

- Explain to pupils exactly what you'll be looking for in the tasks, then mark those points. Don't mark everything in sight.

Homework

- 'Target' mark books on a rotational basis – less weight to carry and you'll be able to offer more comprehensive and meaningful feedback.

- Get pupils to mark their own work – an ideal opportunity for self-assessment and instant feedback.

- Get pupils to peer mark – instant feedback and an idea of how the pupils are doing in comparison to others.

- Mark work during class time – whilst checking pupils' class work, you could check their homework, and give them instant feedback.

Some of the above ideas may be completely inappropriate for some classes. You'll need to find out what works for them as well as for you.

12

Extending Opportunity: A National Framework for Study Support

This is a relatively recent government development and, as such, is a bit of an unknown quantity. There is no doubt that, if it is effective, it will alleviate the burden on teachers and schools with regard to homework.

What is it?

Homework clubs (facilities and support); help with key skills, including literacy, numeracy and ICT; study clubs (linked to or extending curriculum subjects); sports, games and adventurous outdoor activities; creative ventures (music, dance, film, drama and the full range of arts); residential events – study weekends and weeks; space and support for coursework and examination revision; opportunities for volunteering activities in the school or community; opportunities to pursue particular interests (science, ICT, law, archaeology, languages); mentoring by adults or other pupils; learning about learning (thinking skills, accelerated learning); community service (crime prevention initiatives, environmental clubs).

Homework

Why it's needed

Success for young people cannot rely purely on good schools and good teaching. Homework and self-directed learning are seen as vital too, because they: increase self-esteem; increase motivation; improve learning habits; lead to independent, lifelong learning; can make the difference between success and failure at school and in later life; offer the opportunity to encounter subjects not taught in school; give mentoring responsibilities.

Your role

To make sure you know what is available in your area; ensure that all the pupils, but especially those who'll benefit most, are aware of local facilities.

Out-of-hours study support in schools

You may be involved in these and, as such, are open to scrutiny from Ofsted. Here is a checklist to help you cover yourself:

◆ How familiar are you with the nature of the homework that has been set?

◆ Do you have a built-in opportunity to give feedback to the teacher who has set the work?

◆ Do you monitor attendance?

◆ Does it tend to be those who would benefit most who are least likely to attend?

Part Two

**Victoria's Resource Bank –
The Very Best**

13

The Power of the Web

The second part of this guide provides teachers with a 'resource bank', containing information on the very best websites to help you set your students inspiring and unusual homework tasks. We all know that the Internet is a tremendously valuable resource at our fingertips, but at the same time we shouldn't forget that it's all too easy for us to use it badly – to spend hours surfing aimlessly or to fritter away precious time on sites which are clearly rather short on facts!

The following selection of websites is broken up into three distinct sections – those websites which really are the bees-knees in terms of homework and can certainly be recommended to your students; top 10 websites broken down by subject; and, finally, a small selection of sites relating to business and personal finance, PSHE and social sciences.

I do hope you'll find my 'resource bank' useful!

14

Helpful Websites:
The Pick of the Bunch

Many of the sites in the following pages are appropriate to recommend to your pupils. However, here are some of the very best sites for homework.

Homework High *www.channel4.com/homework*
Kevin's Playroom *www.kevinsplayroom.co.uk*

An award-winning homework help site.

SOS Teacher *www.bbc.co.uk/schools/sosteacher*

15

Top 10 Websites for Each Subject

Art

24 Hour Museum   *www.24hourmuseum.org.uk*
A portal to more than 2,500 museum, gallery and heritage sites. Includes: updated search facility; sections for teachers; online exhibitions; newsletters.

AccessArt   *www.accessart.org.uk*
Easy access to contemporary issues in visual arts; exchange of information and ideas; a creative fun learning tool for students in all key stages.

Artworks   *www.art-works.org.uk*
The website of the Vivien Duffield foundation which distributes prizes worth £45,000 to individuals and schools; information about every gallery in the country; a 'virtual' gallery of prize winners.

BBC Artzone   *www.bbc.co.uk/arts*
Interviews with artists; the uses of bad art in the twentieth century; a section on art networks.

Design Council   *www.design-council.org.uk*
Ideas about online design; details of bursaries and grants for students; news of Design in Education Week.

The Incredible Art Department   *www.artswire.org*
Interactive art room; art news; chat; cartoons; lesson plans; an art site of the week.

National Curriculum – Art and Design   *www.nc.uk.net*

Homework

Reasons why art and design are on the National Curriculum; requirements at all four key stages.

Ofsted: The Arts Inspected. *www.ofsted.gov.uk/artsinsp*
Case studies of good teaching practice; audio and visual materials; downloadable materials for use in schools; extensive appendices.

Schemes of Work: Primary/Secondary Art and Design
www.standards.dfes.gov.uk/schemes2/art/?view=get
www.standards.dfee.gov.uk/schemes2/secondary_art
Guidance; resource units; online teachers' guide.

Tate   *www.tate.org.uk*
Covers: Tate Modern; Tate Britain; Tate Gallery Liverpool; Tate Gallery St. Ives; The Turner Collection. Online archive of 8,000 images and 25,000 words.

Design and Technology

BBC Food   *www.bbc.co.uk/food*
A comprehensive site that will bombard you with ideas.

Design Museum   *www.designmuseum.org*
A showcase for the best in contemporary design; a range of downloadable teachers' packs on design innovators and movements; 'Digital Design Museum' shows examples of cutting-edge digital graphics and web design.

D&T Online   *www.dtonline.org/intro.htm*
Free access to design and technology software for pupils to use alongside the National Curriculum; currently targeted at Key Stages 3 and 4, but some aspects will appeal to Key Stage 2 pupils; some sections relevant to Science and Mathematics.

The Design and Technology Association
www.data.org/welcome
A professional association for all involved in design and

technology education; aims to 'support, encourage, promote, develop and maintain design and technological education in all its branches'; includes extracts from the *Journal of Design and Technology Education.*

How Stuff Works   *www.howstuffworks.com*
Informative essays explain everyday technology, from steam engines to combination locks and food; extensive list of subjects with seemingly endless links.

KentEd *www.kented.org.uk/ngfl/sendat/downloads.html*
A vast array of teaching ideas; projects that would be ideal for homework, ranging from making boats and bird food to masks and puppets, all of which ideas are free.

Ofsted: Inspecting Design and Technology 11-16
www.ofsted.gov.uk/publications/index.cfm?fuseaction= pubs.summary&id=1053
Ofsted's guide to help inspectors, headteachers and staff to evaluate design and technology for pupils aged 11-16, with advice on self-evaluation.

Primary/Secondary schemes of work: design and technology
www.standards.dfes.gov.uk/schemes2/designtech/?view= get
www.standards.dfes.gov.uk/schemes2/secondary_det
Guidance on schemes of work; 27 resource units for teachers to download and use or adapt as they wish.

Technology Student   *www.technologystudent.com*
Aimed at teachers and students; offers a wealth of useful material on subjects including: vocational work, drawing techniques, PCB work.

Vegetarian Society's School Room   *www.vegsoc.org*
Primary and secondary resources. 'Primary Project Pack' comprises: lesson plans, activity sheets. At primary level,

deals with: food chains, salad plants, sprouting, nutrition, fibre, protein. At secondary level, deals with: nutritional information, menu planners and recipes. Information on: soya, tofu, TVP, gelling agents, chilled desserts.

Drama and Music

Andrew McCann's Drama Workshop
www.dramateachers.co.uk
A collection of ideas for teaching drama and developing language skills.

BBC Parents' Music Room
www.bbc.co.uk/music/parents
Includes advice and curriculum support.

Classical Composers Database
www.classical-composers.org
A large directory covering 2,000 composers with brief biographical details and links to relevant websites.

Classical Net   *www.classical.net*
Links to thousands of classical music sites.
Over 2,000 CD reviews.

Music at School   *www.musicatschool.co.uk*
Resources and Internet links for secondary school music study. Downloadable worksheets and schemes of work with online quizzes.

Music Teachers' Resource Site   *www.mtrs.co.uk*
Packed with useful information and links. Teachers' reviews of musical instruments; MIDI files; 'Ask An Expert' panel.

National Drama   *www.nationaldrama.co.uk*
The site for professional drama teachers at all levels, including teacher educators, student teachers, advisers, consultants, educational theatre workers and teachers of those with special needs.

Top 10 Websites for Each Subject

Shakespeare's Globe   *www.shakespeares-globe.org*
Includes an extensive education section.

Theatre Museum   *www.theatremuseum.vam.ac.uk*
Part of the Victoria and Albert and the National Grid for Learning; education programme includes workshops relating to the National Curriculum and all aspects of drama.

Virtual Drama Studio   *www.thevirtualdramastudio.co.uk*
Resources for teaching drama and theatre studies to pupils at secondary level.

English

ABC tales   *www.youngABCtales.com*
Hosted by Terry Deary (*Horrible Histories*); encourages children to publish their short stories and poems; free resource pack for teachers.

British Library   *www.education.bl.uk*
Six projects: 'Displaying the Written Word', 'Getting the Message Across', 'Victorian Britain', 'Special Books', 'Newspapers', 'Traditional Stories'; lesson plans; teachers' zone; children's zone.

The English and Media Centre
www.englishandmedia.co.uk
Support for teachers and students of English and Media Studies: recent news; publications catalogue; sample pages; archive of *The English and Media Magazine*; sign up for newsletters and free material; information about the centre's subscription website, with more than 2,000 pages of teaching resources and a fully searchable database of reviews (*www.emextra.com*).

The English Association   *www.le.ac.uk/engassoc*
An English language and literature website, which aims to foster good practice in its teaching and learning at all levels.

Homework

FRET: Free Resources for English Teaching
www.english-teaching.co.uk
Does what it says for teachers at secondary level: lesson plans; schemes of work; organized according to National Curriculum orders for English, covering: reading (poetry, prose, drama, media, non-fiction), writing, speaking, listening.

National Reading Campaign *www.readon.org.uk*
Promotes reading through a series of themes aimed at different age groups; the 'Reading Champions' campaign aims to celebrate those who have acted as positive male role models for reluctant readers.

The Poetry Society *www.poetrysociety.org.uk*
Aims to: boost literacy skills, instil an early appreciation of poetry, resources, National Poetry Day; poetry competitions.

The Shakespeare Insulter
www.pangloss.com/seide/Shaker
An endless supply of the bard's venom.

Talking to Shakespeare *www.talkingto.co.uk*
Unusual insights into the life and work of: William Shakespeare, Charles Dickens, Jane Austen, Virginia Woolf, Thomas Hardy, George Orwell.

Teachit *www.teachit.co.uk*
A growing library of classroom resources and schemes of work by and for secondary teachers; over 1,500 free and downloadable (PDF format) items.

Geography

The European Children's Trust
www.everychild.org.uk
Takes Key Stage 2 children on a virtual tour of Moldova, where they find out how changes in its climatic, economic and political situation affect the lives of the children who

live there. Packed with activities and downloadable material; access is free.

GCSE Bitesize: Geography
www.bbc.co.uk/schools/gcsebitesize
Interactive site allows students to revise the main concepts in bitesize chunks and then tests their knowledge. Topics covered include: tectonics; ecosystems; weather; population; cities. Also includes questions that can be put to a teacher and tips from students from previous years.

The Geographical Association *www.geography.org.uk*
Ideas for persuading students to (continue to) study geography; project ideas.

Georesources *www.georesources.co.uk*
A wide range of geography resources and links, which include: virtual fieldwork; case studies; maps; digital photography; homework project ideas; quizzes; teachers' page; links to exam boards, publishers and other useful organizations.

Global Gang *www.globalgang.org*
A Christian website which links up children from all over the world, including those from countries such as: Brazil; Afghanistan; the Democratic Republic of Congo. Contains: photographs; video clips; stories; letters; features. A section called 'Planet Teacher' includes: activity sheets; cross-curricular material. Background information on issues like: Fair Trade; refugees; children's rights. 'Homework Help' explores topics such as: water; a village in India; aspects of health.

Metlink International Weather Project
www.atschool.eduweb.co.uk/radgeog/MetNetEur/Met-NetEur.html
The Royal Meteorological Society runs an annual Internet weather project for primary and secondary schools worldwide, in January and February. Teachers and pupils make

and exchange weather information on a daily basis for two weeks. With the help of meteorological professionals, they analyse and interpret the data.

Online Atlas for Children   *www.childrensatlas.com*
Develops map-reading and information-handling skills; aimed at primary school children.

Ordnance Survey   *www.mapzone.co.uk*
Aimed at Key Stage 3; allows students to: develop basic mapping skills; use maps for finding information. An interactive and animated child's bedroom acts as an interface between the following sections: 'MapAbility' – guides children through eight core mapping skills, including how to use grid references, understanding scale, hard-to-take compass bearings; 'MapSchool' – two map-based mini-projects: glaciation in Snowdonia and the development of a coastal town in the north of England; 'MapTivity' – quizzes, themed games, resources; 'MapBuilder' – a multimedia mapping tool that enables children to design and build their own maps of the UK, Europe and the world.

Water in the School   *www.waterintheschool.co.uk*
Tells children how to: monitor their school's water use; think about ways of reducing consumption; save money; help the environment. Links into: Maths; Literacy; Science; Technology; Environmental studies.

Young Transnet   *www.youngtransnet.org.uk*
Aims to make improvements for young people in: walking; cycling; public transport. Acts as a platform for children's opinions and suggestions about transport in their area; can be used to analyse their journey to school. Information submitted to the site is accessed by local travel planners and can be used by schools for material to be used in: Geography; Citizenship; ICT; Maths.

Top 10 Websites for Each Subject

History

Active History   *www.activehistory.co.uk*
Useful source of online activities and resources to help bring history alive; suitable for Years 7–13.

BBC Education Online: History for Schools
www.bbc.co.uk/webguide/schools/subcat.shtml?history
Primary, secondary and post-16 levels; links to many sites, including some offering hands-on activities; updated weekly.

Black History Month   *www.black-history-month.co.uk*
This is held every October and promotes knowledge of black history and experience with information on positive black contributions to British society. The site aims to heighten the confidence and awareness of black people in their cultural heritage. There are 400 events held in Britain. See also Acts of Achievement (*www.actsofachievement.org.uk*).

Channel 4's History Site   *www.channel4.com/history*
'Time Travellers' Guides to Stuart England and Tudor England', with a game where students must use their knowledge of the Armada to stay afloat; guides to Mediaeval Britain and the Roman Empire; Black and Asian history map of the UK; 'Time Team', with an archaeological detective game; forum for debate and opinion; 'History Heads' section with opinion pieces; links to 'Homework High', 'History Quest' and appropriate parts of channel4.com/learning.

Children's Compass
www.thebritishmuseum.ac.uk/childrenscompass
Hosted by Alfred the British Museum lion; aimed at children aged 7–11; information on more than 800 key objects in the British Museum. Children can do a variety of activities, including: solve the hieroglyph's spell; open the mummy's

Homework

tomb; piece together the Sutton Hoo helmet; design a mythical creature; follow an online tour about animal mummies; get art and writing work displayed; special tours for younger children. The search facility simplifies the finding of groups of objects related to a theme, period or place.

Fallen Heroes   *www.fallenheroes.co.uk*
A school's research on the First World War.

Historic Royal Palaces   *www.hrp.org.uk*
A site about: HM Tower of London; Hampton Court Palace; Kensington Palace; the Banqueting House at Whitehall. Visitor information; historical facts; images.

The Learning Curve   *www.learningcurve.pro.gov.uk*
The National Archives Learning Curve ties in with the History National Curriculum for Key Stages 2–5. Large range of original sources, including: documents; photo-graphs; film; sound recordings. Exhibitions provide in-depth information, organized into galleries; interactive activities; teachers' notes.

The National Trust
www.nationaltrust.org.uk/historicproperties
Subdivided into categories, such as: architecture; collec-tions; loans; conservation. Visitors to the site can research anything from crenellated castles to crinolines.

Revise for GCSE with the History Channel
www.thehistorychannel.co.uk
GCSE revision quiz. Topics include: Plains Indians; public health; the Russian Revolution; the history of medicine; Vietnam; causes of World War II; League of Nations; the Industrial Revolution; Hitler's Germany and the Cold War. Each topic has a key facts section and a range of quizzes. Other features of the 'Classroom' section include: more than 40 curriculum-related GCSE articles; a student debating chamber; exam tips.

Top 10 Websites for Each Subject

ICT

Bletchley Park *www.bletchleypark.org.uk*
A site about the building where the first programmable computer was built and the German armed forces' top secret codes were broken during World War II.

British Educational Communications and Technology Agency *www.becta.org.uk/index.cfm*
Offers educational support services.

Curriculum *www.curriculum.org.uk*
Users can register and gain free access to resources designed to help promote creative teaching in ICT.

DfES – The Standards Site *www.standards.dfes.gov.uk*
Materials and guidance on the IT Scheme of Work. Teachers can download units in Word and cut and paste text to meet their particular needs.

Everything ICT
www.totalasp.co.uk/default2.asp?tree=131
A portal of resources for GCSE and A-level courses.

ICT GCSE *www.itgcse.org.uk*
Project guides; tips; exercises; quizzes and animations.

Icteachers *www.icteachers.co.uk*
Organized into topics, including: electricity; forces; shadows; plants; habitats; materials; the Earth in space.

Learning and Teaching Scotland *www.ltscotland.org.uk*
Resources for schools and colleges; links to other educational sources.

Mr Jennings *www.mrjennings.co.uk*
Recommended by the National Grid for Learning. Ideas on how to involve parents; materials; homework plans.

Homework

Teach ICT *www.teach-ict.com*
Teaching materials; links; updated daily.

Mathematics

Association of Teachers of Mathematics
www.atm.org.uk
Encourages the enjoyment of maths; helps the understanding of how people learn maths; shares and evaluates teaching and learning strategies; promotes new ideas and possibilities.

Crocodile Mathematics
www.crocodileclips.com/crocodile/mathematics/index.html
Software that allows students to create their own maths laboratory; 80 free lesson plans for Key Stages 3 and 4.

Centre for the Popularisation of Mathematics
www.cpm.informatics.bangor.ac.uk/centre
Two intriguing websites: 'Symbolic Sculpture and Mathematics' explores the interrelation of art and maths and 'Mathematics and Knots' is an Internet version of a travelling exhibition. Both sites include: photographs; diagrams and animated images.

Fibonacci Numbers and Nature *www.mcs.surrey.ac.uk/ Personal/R.Knott/Fibonacci/fibnat.html*

History of Mathematics Archive
http://www-history.mcs.st-and.ac.uk/history
Amongst the items are: 'Famous curves'; a chronology of the history of maths; mathematicians of the day; material on Edinburgh Mathematician James Clerk Maxwell.

Maths Lessons *www.mymaths.co.uk*
A fun revision site for Key Stages 3 and 4.

Mathematics Enrichment Club *www.nrich.maths.org*
Free mathematical puzzles, covering all key stages.

Top 10 Websites for Each Subject

MathsNet *www.mathsnet.net*
Resources for teaching maths, information technology and the Internet.

National Curriculum for Maths *www.nc.uk.net*
The structure and requirements of the National Curriculum for Maths. Information for Key Stages 1–4 on: implementation dates; attainment targets; programmes of study.

Top Maths *www.clickteaching.com*
A site for primary teachers, which includes: tips and ideas; worksheets; advice; a dictionary of maths jargon.

Media

BAFTA *www.bafta.org*
Developments in film, TV and interactive media.

The BBC *www.bbc.co.uk*
BBC News *www.bbc.co.uk/news*
BBC Newsround *www.bbc.co.uk/cbbcnews*
News stories; quizzes; competitions; discussion boards.

British Board of Film Classification *www.cbbfc.co.uk*
Shows why and how the BBFC classifies films, videos, DVDs and some games; information for parents and teachers.

Channel 4 *www.channel4.co.uk*

Film Education *www.filmeducation.org*
Online material complements its study guides and CD-Roms relating to new and classic films.

Ideasfactory *www.ideasfactory.tv*
Promotes awareness of careers in the creative industries.

ITN *www.itn.co.uk*

Homework

National Museum of Photography, Film and Television
www.nmpft.org.uk
Includes educational resources for all key stages.

The Reuters Foundation   *www.foundation.reuters.com*
Supports a range of journalism and information technology
educational projects around the world.

SkyTV   *www.sky.com*

Modern Languages

Adopt an Escargot   *www.adoptanescargot.com*
A fun site covering basic vocabulary and phrases.

Bonjour   *www.bonjour.org.uk*
A self-study site, which covers less ground than other sites
but is nonetheless excellent. Reading passages include
profiles on *South Park* characters and football heroes; facility
to click on difficult vocabulary for an instant translation; form-
filling practice in the 'Matchmaking' zone; GCSE speaking
questions with model answers; a virtual tutor available to
help. Includes lessons for younger learners, which are
imaginatively structured to progress from vocabulary recogni-
tion to active use, or useful for older pupils revising the basics.

BBC Languages
www.bbc.co.uk/education/languages/french
www.bbc.co.uk/education/languages/german
www.bbc.co.uk/education/languages/spanish
Beginners' material in French, German and Spanish.

Foreign Language Resource Centre Links
www.unc.edu
Links to selected sites, covering: literature; newspapers;
magazines; radio; television; dictionaries. Lessons in:
French; Spanish; Italian; Portuguese; Catalan.

Top 10 Websites for Each Subject

Gut! *www.languageskills.co.uk*
Comprehensive set of interactive activities with 200 exercises, some with audio samples of native German speakers.

Learn *www.learn.co.uk*
GCSE support cards, classified by topic area; links to relevant websites tied into Schemes of Work; 'Lessons and Tests' section, including: vocabulary lists, interactive exercises, reading, speaking and writing materials, extensive grammar section.

Learn Spanish *www.studyspanish.com*
Lots of free material; excellent sound quality; vocabulary lists followed by a range of interactive exercises and a grammar section with quizzes; online translator.

L'escale *www.lescale.net*
An action-packed site that encourages young explorers to investigate an island and discover buried treasure.

Linguaweb *www.linguaweb.co.uk*
Covers: French; Spanish; German; Italian (limited). Roughly equivalent to GCSE standard. Listening; speaking; reading; writing; revision club, including reading passages and interactive exercises.

Zut! *www.languageskills.co.uk*
Hundreds of activities, including: jumbled sentences; word searches; listening exercises; dialogues. Organized by year group and subdivided into topics.

PSHE

Anne Frank Trust UK *www.annefrank.org.uk*
Resources include 'Moral Courage – Who's Got It?' Primary and secondary teachers' pack; guidelines for teaching: citizenship, human rights, democracy.

Homework

Citizenship Calendar
www.citizenship-global.org.uk/calendar.html
Events for teaching and discussion; links to further
information; resources; activity ideas.

Development Education Association   *www.dea.org.uk*
Classroom resources and website materials; details of black
and ethnic minority organizations.

Everyone is Equal   *www.equalcitizen.org.uk*
Aimed at Key Stages 3 and 4. Deals with: gender
stereotypes; decision-making; equal pay; work-life balance;
caring, bullying; responsibility for contraception.

Mind, Body and Soul Site for Teenagers
www.mindbodysoul.gov.uk
Aimed at Key Stage 4. Up-to-date information about drugs,
alcohol and mental health; medical conditions explained:
acne, ME, diabetes, asthma and anaphylaxis; links to at
least 100 other health websites.

Oxfam: Cool Planet for Kids *www.oxfam.org/coolplanet*
Teaches about countries in which Oxfam works. Online
quizzes, Fair Trade recipes; teacher advisory zone.

The Samaritans   *www.samaritans.org*
'Youth Pack' covers discussion points and roles plays.
Chapters include: fear; isolation, depression, self-harm and
suicide.

Save the Children   *www.savethechildren.org.uk*
Offers a different perspective on refugees, based on
photographs of young Palestinians living in camps.

SchoolNet Global   *www.schoolnetglobal.com*
A children's contributory website. Children write about their
lives, families and communities; helps children to understand
people of other generations, backgrounds and cultures.

Trashed   *www.trashed.co.uk*
Comprehensive, objective information about drugs and the consequences of their use; medical, social and legal viewpoints.

Religious Education

Baptist Union of Great Britain   *www.baptist.org*
Who they are; beliefs; Baptist roots; the Baptist family.

The Church of England   *www.cofe.anglican.org*
History, structure and beliefs.

Good Questions, Good Answers on Buddhism
www.buddhanet.net/qanda.htm
Basic information in a question-and-answer format.

Hinduism for Schools – Vivekananda Centre, London
www.btinternet.com/ ~ vivakananda/schools
Support and help for GCSE and A-level teachers.

International Catholic Weekly   *www.cathport.com*
A portal with links to Catholic-related sites around the world. Indexed by region and country; list of top 10 UK Catholic websites.

Judaism 101   *www.jewfaq.org*
Online encyclopaedia of Judaism. People; places; language; scripture; holidays; practices and customs.

The Methodist Church of Great Britain
www.methodist.org.uk
Beliefs, structure and history.

Pagan Federation   *www.paganfed.org*
Information about the history of paganism and modern pagans.

Homework

Russian Orthodox Church
www.russian-orthodox-church.org.ru
History, role today, mission and organisation.

Understanding Islam and Muslims *www.islamicity.com*
Leads to basic facts and figures about the Islamic faith, customs and beliefs.

Science

Auriga Astronomy   *www.auriga-astronomy.com*
Covers various areas of the curriculum. Downloadable audio files; teaching aids.

Chemical Elements   *www.chemicalelements.com*
Created by a student.

Dragonfly   *www.units.muohio.edu/dragonfly*
Aimed at Key Stages 1 and 2. Promotes enquiry-based learning. Advice for pupils and teachers on investigations; the chance to interact with experienced researchers; extensive use of photos and illustrations; good selection of video and audio files; forum area for parents and teachers; easy navigation; covers many aspects of the curriculum.

NASA   *www.grc.nasa.gov*
A veritable plethora of stimulating resources. Includes STAR (Science through Arts) project, a multi-disciplinary, multi-lingual, science-based ICT project.

NoiseNet   *www.noisenet.ws*
For Key Stages 3–5. Aims to raise awareness of science and engineering among teenagers. Focuses on how everyday life is affected by science. Provides examples such as skateboarding, surfing, global warming and coastal erosion; items on travel, sport, fashion, entertainment and the environment; brief biographies of young scientists who could be regarded as role models.

Top 10 Websites for Each Subject

Planet Science *www.planet-science.com*
A colourful, lively site. Games; a science room; amazing facts; quizzes; competitions; features.

Science Active *www.science-active.co.uk*
Aimed at Key Stages 3–5. Covers various aspects of science, including experimental and investigative science. Multimedia activities; downloadable materials, including PowerPoint presentations and worksheets; quizzes; support cards; animations; movie of the day; easy navigation; well presented.

Science Line *www.sciencenet.org.uk*
Answers any scientific questions; database of frequently asked questions; online response service.

Science Teacher Stuff *www.scienceteacherstuff.com*
For Key Stages 3 and 4. Portal designed to save teachers' time on the Internet. Resources are grouped under science headings: life; earth, physical, space and environmental; covers wider aspects of science such as safety, teaching strategies and assessment.

Try Science *www.tryscience.co.uk*
For Key Stages 1–4. Links to more than 400 science and technology centres worldwide; experiments section for offline activities; parent and teacher pages.

16

Useful Websites for Other Subjects

Business and Personal Finance

Britannic Street   *www.britannicstreet.co.uk*
A soap-opera-type video to teach Key Stage 4 students the basics of personal finance. Covers topics such as planning for retirement and living away from home.

The Personal Finance Education Group *www.pfeg.org*
Helps to develop financial capability in young people. Directory of resources, classified according to age and key stage of children and teaching resources linked to DfES curriculum guidance. Many free resources, including: *Maths Counts* (Key Stages 1 and 2); 10 games centred on supermarket shopping, covering numeracy as well as themes of financial capability; *Budgeting for Beginners* (Key Stages 2-4) which deals with basic budgeting through scenarios, printable personal budget monitoring tasks, interactive programmes; *Pro Share Student Investor* (Key Stages 3 and 4), a pack of 10 activities to develop students' understanding of shares and the risks involved in preparation for the ProShare Forecast challenge; *Your Money Be Wise* (Key Stage 3 onwards), a paper-based resource for teaching practical financial skills with case studies, giving practical examples of personal finance in action.

Today's Preparation for Tomorrow's Vision: Support for teachers for business studies
www.micro-active.com/tptv
Targets all levels, from newly qualified teachers to heads of

Useful Websites for Other Subjects

departments. New practical teaching and learning strategies; examples of materials for all levels.

Tutor2u *www.tutor2u.net*
A portal for students and teachers of economics. Study guides; revision notes and news; discussion forum; modified by a network of experienced teachers.

Young Money *www.young-money.co.uk*
Web-based quiz show about managing money.

General

Learn *www.learn.co.uk*
A general resource for all levels from *The Guardian*. An excellent GCSE revision resource.'Six of the Best' provides links to relevant websites, tied in to schemes of work.

Teacher Resource Exchange *www.tre.ngfl.gov.uk*
Allows teachers to share and develop teaching resources and activities.

Vertude Reality *www.vertude.co.uk*
Provides packs of activity worksheets for every curriculum subject from ages 5–18.

Physical Education

Blue Dome *www.bluedome.co.uk*
Up-to-date information on adventurous activities and events.

The Physical Education Association of the United Kingdom *www.pea.uk.com*
Advice on all matters relating to PE.

PE Primary *www.peprimary.co.uk*
Contains 150 ideas for gymnastics, dance and games.

Sport England *www.sportengland.org*
Contains 6,000 sporting contacts; information on 4,000

sports facilities; news on major events; lists sports-related educational courses.

Sports Media   *www.sports-media.org*
Lesson plans; handy tips; drills; activities; teaching aids.

Teach PE   *www.TeachPE.com*
Resources for teachers of GCSE and A level, with plenty of interaction.

Social Sciences

The Association for the Teaching of the Social Sciences
www.le.ac.uk/education/centres/ATSS/atss.html
Promotes the teaching and learning of the social sciences at all levels.

European Union   *www.europa.eu.int*
Packed with information about the workings of the European Union. News of inter-governmental negotiations; history; structure; selection of documents and agreements.

Explore Parliament   *www.explore.parliament.uk*
Parliamentary Education Unit. Shows teachers how to use online activities as a teaching resource.

Global Dimension   *www.globaldimension.org.uk*
Free database of over 600 resources. Graded for use by: subject; pupil age and UK curriculum.

Political Parties
Conservatives *www.conservatives.com*
Green Party *www.greenparty.org.uk*
Independence Party *www.independence.org.uk*
Labour *www.labour.org.uk*
Liberal Democrats *www.libdems.org.uk*
Plaid Cymru *www.plaidcymru.org*
SNP *www.snp.org.uk*
UUP *www.uup.org*

Bibliography

Barrett, D.E. and Neal, K.S. (1992) 'Effects of homework assistance given by telephone on the academic achievement of fifth grade children', *Education Research Quarterly* 15(4), 21-8.

Bryan, T. and Sullivan-Burstein, K. (1998) 'Teacher-selected strategies for improving homework completion', *Remedial and Special Education* 19(5), 263-75.

Butler, J.A. (1987) 'Homework', School Improvement Research Series, Northwest Regional Educational Laboratory: Portland.

Chavous, B.J. (1996) 'A study of teacher and student attitudes toward a program utilising a calendar of homework activity', *National Association of Laboratory Schools Journal* 15(1), 22-9.

Clark, C., Clark, F. and Vogel, M. (1989) *Hassle-free Homework*, Doubleday: New York.

Cooper, H. (1989) *Homework*, Longman: New York.

Cooper, H. (1994) *The Battle over Homework: An Administrator's Guide to Setting Sound and Effective Policies*, Corwin Press: Newsbury Park.

Corno, L. (1996) 'Homework is a complicated thing', *Educational Researcher* 25(8), 27-39.

Kravolec, E. and Buell, J. (2000) *The End of Homework: How Homework Disrupts Family Life, Overburdens Children, and Limits Learning*, Beacon Press: Boston.

Paulu, N. (1995) *Helping your Students with Homework: A Guide for Teachers*, Office of Educational Research, US Department of Education: Washington.

Homework

Reese, R. (1997) 'Homework: What does the Research Say?', *www.ericps.crc.uiuc.edu*

Sharp, C. et al. (2001) *Homework: A Review of Recent Research*, National Foundation for Educational Research: Slough.